PLAY & LEARN MATH
Hundred Chart
Learning Games and Activities to Help Build Foundational Math Skills

by Susan Andrews Kunze

New York • Toronto • London • Auckland • Sydney
Mexico City • New Delhi • Hong Kong • Buenos Aires

Editor: Maria L. Chang
Cover design by Tannaz Fassihi
Cover art by Constanza Basaluzzo
Interior design by Grafica Inc.
Interior art by Mike Moran

Scholastic Inc., 557 Broadway, New York, NY 10012
ISBN: 978-1-338-26474-6
Copyright © 2019 by Susan Andrews Kunze
All rights reserved.
Printed in the U.S.A.
First printing, January 2019.
1 2 3 4 5 6 7 8 9 10   40   25 24 23 22 21 20 19

Contents

Introduction

Walk into any primary-grade classroom, and you're sure to find a hundred chart displayed on the wall. This simple, inexpensive tool is readily available online, in teacher stores, and in many mathematics programs' teaching guides. Yet, surprisingly, this potentially rich resource is often underutilized in the classroom. Teachers typically use them to practice counting, do skip counting, or look for patterns—but not much more beyond that.

Play & Learn Math: Hundred Chart offers numerous ways to incorporate hundred charts into your instruction for a variety of math concepts. This compilation of activities is designed to help children gain mathematical understanding and practice using individual hundred charts (also known as hundred boards). These activities do not require hundred boards with number tiles or a wall chart, but are designed for hands-on work with easy-to-find tools.

The activities in this book are grouped into sections based on the mathematics concepts they most directly address. They span concepts and skills taught in 1st through 3rd grades. Most of them have strong pattern recognition and problem-solving components. You may be surprised to see many "simple" activities provide exceptional practice in higher-level thinking skills. I have tested these activities over nearly four decades of teaching in my own elementary classroom and in the classrooms of teachers with whom I've shared my discoveries.

Almost every activity in this book is written in two ways: one to guide teachers on how to implement the activity, and another to give children instructions using kid-friendly language. The purpose of this is simple—the teacher introduces the activity to the whole class or to small groups, then children can use their own copy, written at their reading level, as a step-by-step reminder of how to play. *Play & Learn Math: Hundred Chart* is ideal for math centers and small groups, in which children can work independently to improve their skills and develop concept understanding.

Most of the activities require a few simple materials, such as plastic chips or other markers. You'll find reproducible Tens and Ones spinners (page 63) at the back of this book, but you can also use number cubes and ten-sided dice if you have them readily available. Activities are also not limited to use on a basic 1–100 chart. To help young children make the leap to understandings beyond 100, many teachers use 1–120 charts. To provide more advanced children with practice with larger numbers, use charts with multiple hundreds or even thousands. Using a 201–300 chart with these activities, for example, provides children with greater challenge and extends understanding.

So now you are ready to start guiding your students in powerful mathematics learning. Children will love these activities, and so will you. Let's get playing!

Mathematics Standards Correlations*

	Patterns in the 100 Chart	Number Neighbors	1-100 Bingo	Number Puzzle	Stamp a 100 Chart	Blocks	Arrows	Pick a Path	Count Off	What's Next?	Clear the Board	Connecting Odd & Even	Place the Numbers	Egg-Carton Toss	Guess the Number	Battleship	Race to 100	Race From 100	What's the Sum?	Innies and Outies	Boxes	Crosses	Patterns in Multiples	Choose & Multiply	Dividing Evenly
GRADE 1																									
OA.C.6 Add and subtract within 20, demonstrating fluency for addition and subtraction within 10.																			✓						
NBT.B.2 Understand that the two digits of a two-digit number represent amounts of tens and ones.	✓	✓	✓	✓	✓	✓	✓	✓					✓	✓	✓	✓									
NBT.B.3 Compare two two-digit numbers based on meanings of the tens and ones digits.		✓				✓									✓										
NBT.C.4 Add within 100, including adding a two-digit number and a one-digit number.									✓	✓								✓							
NBT.C.5 Given a two-digit number, mentally find 10 more or 10 less than the number, without having to count; explain the reasoning used.		✓																							
NBT.C.6 Subtract multiples of 10 in the range 10–90 from multiples of 10 in the range 10–90 using concrete models or drawings and strategies based on place value, properties of operations, and/or the relationship between addition and subtraction.		✓																							
GRADE 2																									
OA.B.2 Fluently add and subtract within 20 using mental strategies.									✓																
OA.C.3 Determine whether a group of objects (up to 20) has an odd or even number of members.	✓								✓			✓		✓	✓								✓		
NBT.A.1 Understand that the three digits of a three-digit number represent amounts of hundreds, tens, and ones.					✓								✓	✓	✓	✓									
NBT.A.3 Read and write numbers to 1000 using base-ten numerals, number names, and expanded form.			✓	✓	✓																				
NBT.B.5 Fluently add and subtract within 100 using strategies based on place value, properties of operations, and/or the relationship between addition and subtraction.						✓	✓	✓	✓	✓	✓						✓	✓	✓	✓	✓	✓			
NBT.B.8 Mentally add 10 or 100 to a given number 100–900, and mentally subtract 10 or 100 from a given number 100–900.		✓																							
MD.C.8 Solve word problems involving dollar bills, quarters, dimes, nickels, and pennies.					✓																				
GRADE 3																									
OA.A.1 Interpret products of whole numbers, e.g., interpret 5 × 7 as the total number of objects in 5 groups of 7 objects each.																							✓	✓	
OA.A.2 Interpret whole-number quotients of whole numbers, e.g., interpret 56 ÷ 8 as the number of objects in each share when 56 objects are partitioned equally into 8 shares, or as a number of shares when 56 objects are partitioned into equal shares of 8 objects each.																									✓
OA.B.5 Apply properties of operations as strategies to multiply and divide.																								✓	✓
OA.D.9 Identify arithmetic patterns (including patterns in the addition table or multiplication table) and explain them using properties of operations.							✓	✓	✓	✓	✓								✓	✓	✓	✓	✓		

Play & Learn Math: Hundred Chart © Susan Andrews Kunze, Scholastic Inc.

Patterns in the Hundred Chart

The brain loves patterns, and the hundred chart is full of them! Guide young primary-grade children into discovering those patterns to help them develop a strong number sense and place value understanding.

Do this activity with the whole class or in small groups several times, focusing on one or two patterns each time. Children will become more nimble with numbers as they begin to recognize patterns and relationships among the numbers on a hundred chart.

HERE'S HOW

Distribute copies of the Blank 100 Chart to children. Display a copy on the board.

Explain to children that this blank chart will help them learn the numbers 1 to 100 and see patterns in the numbers. Have children start filling in their own chart by writing the numbers 1 to 10 on the top row, beginning with the box on the top left corner and ending with the box on the top right corner. Do the same on the whiteboard chart. Then encourage children to continue filling in the chart on their own up to 25.

Enlist children's help in filling in the rest of the chart. Point to a square and ask: *What do you think goes here?* Guide children to look for patterns in rows and columns. Ask them to:

• notice in which direction the numbers change by one *(left and right)* and in which direction they change by ten *(up and down);*

• look for odd or even numbers;

• identify numbers with the same digits in both ones and tens places;

• search for specific digits in numbers, and so on.

MATERIALS

• Blank 100 Chart (page 61)
• pencils
• classroom projection system or hundred wall chart and markers

VARIATION

For younger students, have them initially write the numbers up to 10 on their blank chart. Then focus on only the first two or three rows when pointing to a blank square and asking them to fill in the missing number.

Number Neighbors

This activity, which can be played with the whole class or in small groups, is a perfect follow-up to finding patterns on the hundred chart. Children determine where to write each number on a blank chart, using its positional relationship to other numbers. This activity strengthens children's number sense and place value understanding.

HERE'S HOW

Distribute copies of the Blank 100 Chart to children.

Start by calling out any number and asking children to locate and write that number on their chart. Then tell children to write in a neighboring number, giving directions such as *one less*, *one more*, *ten less*, or *ten more*, depending on their skill level. For example, say you call out the number 12. After checking that children have correctly located and written 12 on their blank chart, ask them to fill in the number that's "one less" (*11*), or with older children, "ten more" (*22*).

Continue having children fill in one neighboring number at a time until their 100 Chart is full or time runs out. You may have children fill in any remaining blank spaces for homework.

MATERIALS

- **Blank 100 Chart (page 61)**
- pencils
- **100 Chart (page 62), optional**
- **plastic chips, optional**

VARIATIONS

- For younger children, start by calling out a number from 1 to 10 or 20.

- For more advanced students, direct them to add or subtract numbers larger than 1; for example, *4 more, 3 less, 30 more, 20 less.*

- As children do the activity, allow them to check their work against the completed 100 Chart. Support struggling students by providing them with a few plastic chips and the 100 Chart. Children can place a chip on the given number on the chart, then use another chip to move to the neighboring number.

1–100 Bingo

Children get lots of practice in identifying the numbers in each decade (or row) of the hundred chart while playing this fun and engaging bingo game. This whole-class game can also be played in small groups with a student or parent as the caller.

HERE'S HOW

Distribute copies of the Blank 100 Chart to children. Provide them with chips to cover the spaces.

Have children fill in their chart, one row at a time. Tell them to fill in the top row by writing the numbers 1 to 10 in random order (for example, 4, 2, 3, 7, and so on). Continue with each row, writing numbers in that decade in random order.

To play the game, spin the Tens and Ones spinners to make a number from 1 to 100. (For example, if you spin a 2 in the Tens spinner and a 5 in the Ones spinner, you made the number 25. Use 00 for 100.) The caller says the number aloud, and children cover that number on their charts with a chip. Continue playing until a player has covered ten numbers vertically, horizontally, or diagonally on his or her chart. The first player to do so wins the game.

MATERIALS

- Blank 100 Chart (page 61)
- plastic chips (or buttons or coins to cover spaces on the chart)
- Tens and Ones spinners (page 63)

VARIATION

Instead of simply calling out numbers, use number problems (e.g., *how many months in a year* or *how many eggs in a dozen*), money questions, 10 or 1 more or less, and so on.

Number Puzzle

Children cut apart a hundred chart to make puzzle pieces. As they put the pieces back together again, they practice ordering numbers using place value understanding, pattern recognition, as well as adding and subtracting tens and ones.

Keep the puzzles in a "puzzle box" (a shoebox or gift box works well) for an instant math learning center!

HERE'S HOW

Distribute copies of the Blank 100 Chart to children. Ask them to write the numbers 1 to 100 in order to complete their charts.

Have children carefully cut on the lines of their chart to make about seven "puzzle pieces." Tell them to write their name or initials on the back of each of their pieces. Then have each child put his or her puzzle pieces into an envelope.

To play, children swap envelopes with one another. (Alternatively, they can place their envelopes in a puzzle box for others to try.) Each child takes someone else's puzzle and assembles it. After solving a puzzle, a child should sign his or her name on the back of the envelope before returning it to the owner or the puzzle box.

MATERIALS

- **Blank 100 Chart (page 61)**
- **pencils**
- **scissors**
- **envelopes**

Name: _____ Date: _____

Number Puzzle

**How well do you know your numbers?
Put together a puzzle to find out.**

What to Do

1 Fill in your Blank 100 Chart. Write the numbers 1 to 100 in order.

2 Cut your chart along the lines to make about seven puzzle pieces.

3 Sign your name or write your initials on the back of each piece.

4 Place your puzzle pieces in an envelope.

5 Write your name on the envelope.

6 Trade puzzles with a classmate. Or, put your envelope in the puzzle box.

7 Take someone else's puzzle. Put the pieces together.

8 After you solve the puzzle, write your name on the envelope.

9 Put the puzzle pieces back in the envelope. Then return the envelope to its owner or the puzzle box.

10 Take a new puzzle and play again!

You'll Need

★ Blank 100 Chart

★ pencil

★ scissors

★ envelope

Stamp a 100 Chart

This cooperative activity has always been a favorite in my classroom. Children work together in small groups to fill in a large hundred chart using base-ten (place value) or coin stamps. You may fold a large chart paper into a 10-by-10 grid for stamping, but I prefer to use wide butcher paper (the kind used to cover classroom bulletin boards).

HERE'S HOW

Fold the paper or draw lines to create a 10-by-10 grid with squares large enough for children to stamp numbers. Provide children with base-ten or coin stamps and a stamp pad.

Tell children to stamp a unit (one) or penny in the top-left corner box of the grid. On the bottom-right corner, have them stamp one flat hundred in base-ten blocks or a dollar coin or bill. Have children fill in the grid row-by-row to replicate the values on a hundred chart. Challenge them to use the fewest number of stamps to fill each square with the correct number. For example, children should use a quarter and a penny to represent *26*, not 26 pennies or other combination.

TIP

You might want to have children start with a smaller chart (like the Blank 100 Chart) and draw the stamps in the squares. They can then use this chart for reference as they stamp the larger grid paper. For children who need extra support, provide a copy of the 100 Chart so they can check their work.

MATERIALS

- large chart or butcher paper
- base-ten or coin stamps
- stamp pad with ink
- Blank 100 Chart (page 61), optional
- 100 Chart (page 62), optional

VARIATIONS

- Have children stamp each number on a large sticky note and place each note on the correct space on the chart.

- No stamps? Have children use markers to make tally marks to show the number for each square of the hundred chart.

Name: _____ Date: _____

Stamp a 100 Chart

Use stamps to make a different kind of hundred chart.

What to Do

1 Use the stamps to stamp numbers on the chart.

2 Start with the number 1 in the top-left corner of the chart.

3 Fill in each square across the first row in order.

4 Fill in the squares in the next row, and so on. Fill in one row at a time.

5 Use the fewest number of stamps to fill each square with the correct number.

6 Check your work with the 100 Chart.

You'll Need

★ base-ten or coin stamps

★ stamp pad with ink

★ large chart folded or marked into a 10-by-10 grid

★ 100 Chart

Blocks

"Blocks" are random sections of a hundred chart with missing numbers. Rather than filling in an entire chart, children fill in portions of the chart and figure out missing numbers using a variety of patterns (+1, –1, +10, –10, as well as +9, –9, +11, and –11). This activity is another great way to help children understand the relationships among numbers on a hundred chart.

HERE'S HOW

Distribute copies of the "Fill the Blocks" activity page to children. Display a copy on the board.

Tell children that instead of filling out an entire hundred chart, they'll be filling in just "blocks" of it. Guide children through the first Block, thinking aloud as you fill in the first few blank spaces. For example, you might say, *"The number to the right of 14 would be 1 more than 14, so that number is 15."* Or with older students, you might say, *"The number below 5 would be 10 more, so 5 + 10 = 15."*

Have children fill in the rest of the Blocks on their own or with a partner.

TIP

Some children may find it helpful to use a plastic chip to identify missing numbers on the 100 Chart as they work on a Block.

MAKING YOUR OWN BLOCKS

Make your own page of Blocks to give children more practice (or have children make them for partners to fill in). Here are two easy ways:

• The easiest and quickest way is to outline each Block shape on graph paper with a fine marker. Fill in a few numbers on each Block shape to help children get started.

• Use a word-processing application to make a table array. Lighten the grid color and outline each Block shape with a broader line. Then add a few numbers on each Block.

MATERIALS

• **Fill the Blocks activity page (page 15)**
• pencils
• classroom projection system
• 100 Chart (page 62), optional
• plastic chips, optional

Name: _____ Date: _____

Fill the Blocks

Fill in the empty spaces in each Block. Think about how the numbers in a 100 chart relate to one another.

1.
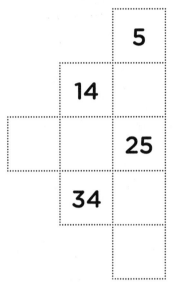

2.
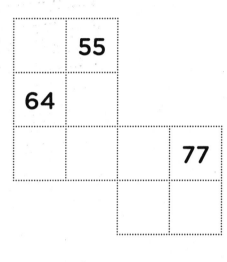

3.

36		38		40
	47			
56				

4.
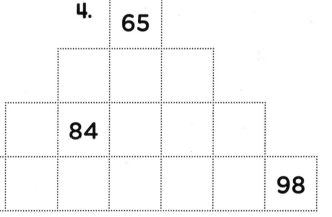

5.
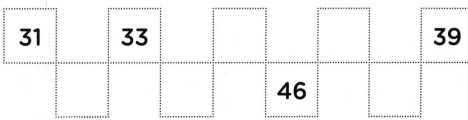

Arrows

"Arrows" is another way to help children understand the relationships among numbers on a hundred chart. Starting from any number, children follow a series of arrows on the 100 Chart to reach an ending number. For example:

7 ↓ ↓ ← ← 25

This activity encourages children to use a variety of patterns—including plus and minus 1, 9, 10, and 11—to find the ending numbers.

HERE'S HOW

Distribute copies of the "Follow the Arrows" activity page to children. Display a copy on the board.

Model how to work the first problem, thinking aloud as you follow the arrows to reach the ending number. For example, you might say, *"Going down from 24, I would have to add 10, so 24 + 10 = 34. I need to add 10 again for the next down arrow, so that's 34 + 10 = 44. To go left from there, I need to subtract 1, so that's 43. I subtract another 1 for the next left arrow, so that's 42. The ending number is 42."*

Have children do the activity on their own or with a partner.

TIP

Some children may find it helpful to use a plastic chip to follow the path of the arrows on the 100 Chart.

MAKE YOUR OWN ARROWS

To make your own page of Arrows, simply hand-draw a set of problems on paper. You can also create a page on any word-processing or drawing application using the arrow feature.

MATERIALS

- Follow the Arrows activity page (page 17)
- pencils
- classroom projection system
- 100 Chart (page 62), optional
- plastic chips, optional

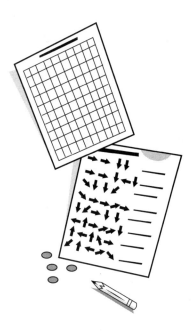

Name:_____ Date:_____

Follow the Arrows

Start with the number on the left.
Then follow the arrows to find the missing number.

1. 24 ↓ ↓ ← ← _____

2. 3 → → ↓ ← ↓ _____

3. 16 ↘ ↓ ↓ ↙ _____

4. 63 ↘ → → ↗ → _____

5. 48 ↓ ↙ ← ↓ ↓ _____

6. 92 ← ↑ → ↗ ↗ ↓ _____

7. 70 ↑ ← ↑ ↖ → _____

8. 55 ↗ ↑ ← ↗ ↘ _____

Pick a Path

This variation of the "Arrows" activity provides both the starting and ending numbers. Children then have to draw a path between the numbers on the 100 Chart. There are multiple paths to get from one number to another. Have children do the activity in pairs so they can check and compare answers with their partner.

HERE'S HOW

Distribute copies of the "Draw the Arrows" activity page and the 100 Chart to children. Display a copy of "Draw the Arrows" on the board.

Model how to work the first problem, thinking aloud as you create a path to reach the ending number. For example, you might say, *"To get from 1 to 34, I need to go down. So let's start with one down arrow, which will get me to 11 [model drawing the arrow on the board]. Another down arrow will get me to 21, and another one will get me to 31. From there, I need to go right, so here's one right arrow, which takes me to 32. Another right lands me on 33, and one more gets me to 34."*

Pair up children and have them work with their partners to do the activity.

TIP

Allow children to move a plastic chip along the path on the 100 Chart to help them with this task.

VARIATION

Pair up children to play "Make Your Own Path," the game version of this activity. Players spin the Tens and Ones spinners to determine the starting and ending numbers. Each player determines a path between the two numbers on the 100 Chart and writes it on his or her "Make Your Own Path" recording sheet. Have partners compare their paths with each other and discuss how the paths are similar and different.

MATERIALS

- Draw the Arrows activity page (page 19)
- 100 Chart (page 62)
- pencils
- plastic chips, optional
- classroom projection system
- Make Your Own Path game directions (page 20), optional
- Make Your Own Path recording sheet (page 21), optional
- Tens and Ones spinners (page 63), optional

Name: _____ Date: _____

Draw the Arrows

Pick a path from the starting number to the ending number. Draw arrows to show direction on the 100 Chart. You can trace the path on the chart with a marker or use a chip to help you.

	Starting Number	Arrows	Ending Number
1.	1		34
2.	56		32
3.	71		98
4.	46		6
5.	68		51
6.	6		35
7.	61		7
8.	80		93

Make Your Own Path

Spin the spinners to get two numbers between 1 and 100. Then make a path between the two numbers.

What to Do

1 Spin the Tens and Ones spinners to get a number.* This is your starting number. Write it on your recording sheet.

2 Spin the spinners again to get another number. This is your ending number. Write it on your recording sheet.

3 Make your own path from the starting number to the ending number. Draw arrows on your 100 Chart. You can use a marker or a plastic chip to help you.

4 Draw the arrows on your recording sheet.

5 Compare your path with your partner's. Are they the same? If not, how are they different?

6 Start again!

Players: 2

You'll Need

★ Tens and Ones spinners

★ Make Your Own Path recording sheet for each player

★ 100 Chart for each player

★ pencil

★ plastic chips or marker (optional)

* For example, if you spin a 2 in the Tens spinner and a 5 in the Ones spinner, your number is 25. 00 means 100.

Play & Learn Math: Hundred Chart © Susan Andrews Kunze, Scholastic Inc.

Name: _____ Date: _____

Make Your Own Path

Spin to make two numbers.
Then draw arrows to make a path between them.

Starting Number	Arrows	Ending Number

Count Off

One of the most common ways to use a hundred chart is to practice skip-counting skills. However, many teachers often forego the important math discussions that can arise from children's discoveries about patterns. This whole-class activity provides opportunities for great math talks to extend student learning. This activity is not meant to be completed in one class period. Focus on one number to skip count at each lesson to ensure children gain a deep understanding of patterns.

HERE'S HOW

Distribute copies of the 100 Chart and highlighters, crayons, or plastic chips to children. Display a copy of the chart on the board.

Decide what number to skip count by. Invite children to count up to that number and color or place a clear chip on the space on their 100 Chart. Have them repeat the process until they reach the end of the chart. For example, say you pick the number 5. Have children count out loud, "1, 2, 3, 4, 5," and color the number 5. (Circle 5 on the 100 Chart on the board.) Counting to 5 again, children color the number 10, then 15, and so on. Have children record the numbers they colored on a sheet of paper or in their math journal. Encourage children to look for any patterns in the numbers they recorded or on the chart.

Take time to discuss patterns children found. Some things they may notice include:

- coloring patterns the skip-counting numbers make. For example, counting by 2s makes a colored/not-colored column pattern. Counting by 3s makes a colored diagonal pattern.

- patterns in the ones digits in the colored numbers. For example, numbers counted by 5s have 5 or 0 in the ones column; numbers counted by 4s have a 4, 8, 2, 6, 0 pattern (e.g., 24, 28, 32, 36, 40, 44, 48, 52, 56, 60).

- even and odd patterns. In some skip-counting patterns, only even numbers get colored. In others, both even and odd numbers are colored. Have children compare several of their skip-counting charts as you ask: *What even number patterns do you see? What odd/even pattern does your skip counting show? Are there any all-odd number patterns?* Compare these odd/even patterns to addition patterns: adding two even numbers equals an even number; adding two odd numbers equals an even number; adding an odd and an even number equals an odd number.

MATERIALS

- 100 Chart (page 62)
- colored highlighters, crayons, or plastic chips
- paper or math journal (for each child)
- classroom projection system

What's Next?

This activity gives children practice with skip counting starting from different numbers. Given a rule and a starting number, children list the next three numbers that follow the rule.

HERE'S HOW

Distribute copies of the "Next Numbers" activity page and the 100 Chart to children, as well as plastic chips. Display a copy of "Next Numbers" on the board.

Point to the headings on the "Next Numbers" activity page: Starting Number, Rule, and What Numbers Come Next? Explain to children that the Starting Number tells them where to start on their 100 Chart, while the Rule tells them what pattern to follow.

Go over the example on the first row of the activity page. Have children place a chip on 21, the starting number, on their 100 Chart. (Circle 21 on the 100 Chart on the board.) Then following the rule of +5, have them count up 5 from 21 to reach 26 and place a chip on that number. (Circle 26 on the board.) Repeat two more times—have children count up 5 again to place a chip on 31, and another one on 36.

Have children complete the activity page on their own or with a partner.

TIP

To support struggling students, have them work with a partner to complete the activity.

MATERIALS

(for each child)

- Next Numbers activity page (page 24)
- 100 Chart (page 62)
- plastic chips
- classroom projection system
- Find What's Next game directions (page 25), optional
- Find What's Next recording sheet (page 26), optional
- Tens and Ones spinners (page 63), optional
- pennies, optional

VARIATION

Pair up children to play "Find What's Next," the game version of this activity. Players use the Tens and Ones spinners to determine the starting number and the rule. Use a penny to determine the operation—heads for addition, tails for subtraction. (For example, if they spin a 5 and the penny lands on heads, the rule is +5.) Players record the starting number and rule on the recording sheet, then list the next three numbers that follow the rule.

Name: _____ Date: _____

Next Numbers

Look at the Starting Number and the Rule. Fill in the next three numbers in each pattern. Use the 100 Chart to help you.

Starting Number	Rule	What Numbers Come Next?		
21	+5	26	31	36
83	−6			
17	+10			
48	−7			
28	+9			
97	−10			
17	+8			
88	−11			
18	+20			
75	−8			
22	+11			

Find What's Next

Make a pattern rule. Then find the numbers that follow that rule.

What to Do

1 Spin the Tens and Ones spinners to get a number. (00 means 100.) This is your starting number. Write it on your recording sheet.

2 Place a chip on that number on your 100 Chart.

3 To get the rule number, spin a spinner. Then flip the penny. "Heads" means <u>add</u> with the rule number. "Tails" means <u>subtract</u> with the rule number. Record the rule on your recording sheet.

4 Follow the rule. Place a chip on the next number on your 100 Chart.

5 Repeat Step 4 to get the next two numbers in the pattern.

6 Record all three numbers on your recording sheet.

7 Compare your numbers with your partner's. Did you get the same numbers? If not, work together to figure out why.

8 Start again!

Players: 2

You'll Need

★ Tens and Ones spinners

★ 100 Chart

★ Find What's Next recording sheet for each player

★ plastic chips

★ penny

Name: _____ Date: _____

Find What's Next

Fill in the starting number and the rule. Then fill in the next three numbers in each pattern. Use the 100 Chart to help you.

Starting Number	Rule	What Numbers Come Next?		
83	**-6**	77	71	65

Clear the Board

"Clear the Board" is another variation of the "What's Next?" activity. In this two-player game, children work in pairs to cover their 100 Chart with plastic chips. Each player then removes four chips at a time following a pattern rule. Using strategy, players choose their own starting number for each play to enable them to remove four plastic chips in the sequence.

HERE'S HOW

Partner up children and give each pair a copy of the 100 Chart and 100 plastic chips. Have partners cover all the numbers on their 100 Chart with chips.

Players agree on a pattern rule,* such as +4 or –7. The first player chooses a starting number and takes off that chip from the 100 Chart. He or she then takes the chips off the next three numbers that follow the pattern rule. The next player then takes a turn.

For example, say the players agree to use the rule "+4." Player 1 chooses and removes the number 9 to start, then 13, 17, and 21. Player 2 chooses and removes the number 41 to start, then 45, 49, and 53.

The game continues until a player cannot take four chips off the board using the rule. The players then count the chips they have collected. The one with the most chips wins the game.

MATERIALS

(for each pair of players)

- **100 Chart** (page 62)**
- **100 plastic chips**

** You may want to laminate the 100 Chart for durability.

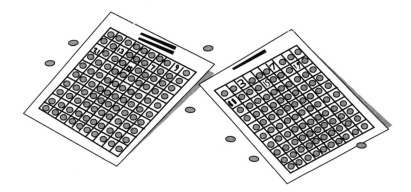

* For a more random way to get the rule, have players spin the Ones spinner (page 63) to get a number, then flip a penny. "Heads" means <u>add</u> with the rule number. "Tails" means <u>subtract</u> with the rule number. For example, if they spin a 3 and the penny lands on tails, the rule is –3.

Clear the Board

Choose a pattern rule. Then clear the board by removing chips from the numbers that follow the rule.

What to Do

1 Cover all the numbers on the 100 Chart with plastic chips.

2 Choose a pattern rule, such as +4 or –7. Decide who goes first.

3 Player 1 picks a starting number. She removes that chip from the 100 Chart. Then she removes the chips from the next three numbers that follow the rule.

Players: 2

You'll Need
★ 100 Chart
★ 100 plastic chips

4 Player 2 takes a turn. He chooses a starting number and removes that chip. Then he removes the chips from the next three numbers that follow the rule.

Here's an example: Say the players choose the rule "+4." Player 1 picks and removes the number 9 to start. Then she removes 13, 17, and 21. Player 2 picks and removes the number 41 to start. Then he removes 45, 49, and 53.

5 Players continue taking turns. At each turn, each player removes four plastic chips from the chart.

6 The game ends when a player cannot remove four chips following the rule.

7 Each player counts his or her chips. The player with the most chips wins.

Connecting Odd & Even

In this fun two-player game, children practice identifying odd and even numbers. To win, players have to choose strategically which odd or even numbers to cover on their 100 Chart. The player who can place five chips in a row—horizontally, vertically, or diagonally—wins.

HERE'S HOW

Partner up children and give each pair a copy of the 100 Chart and a number cube. (If you don't have number cubes, children can use the Ones spinner instead.) Players will use spaces 1–50 on the 100 Chart, so they can either cover the bottom half with a half sheet of paper or draw a line below 50 as a reminder.

Give each player 15 chips of one color. Players take turns rolling the number cube. If a player rolls an even number, he covers any even number on the 100 Chart with a chip. If a player rolls an odd number, she covers any odd number on the chart. The goal is to place five chips in a row—horizontally, vertically, or diagonally. The game continues until one player has placed five chips in a row.

Have players start a new game and continue playing until time is up.

MATERIALS

- 100 Chart* (page 62)
- half sheet of paper
- number cube
- 15 plastic chips of one color for each player

* You may want to laminate the 100 Chart for durability.

VARIATION

Have children play the game on any 50 spaces; for example, 31–80 or 51–100.

Connecting Odd & Even

Find and cover odd or even numbers on the 100 Chart.

What to Do

1 You will play on the top half of the 100 Chart. Use the paper to cover the bottom half of the chart.

2 Players take turns rolling the number cube. The player who gets the higher number goes first.

3 Player 1 rolls the number cube. If the cube lands on an even number, the player places a chip on any even number on the chart. If it lands on an odd number, the player places a chip on any odd number.

4 Player 2 takes a turn and does the same.

5 The goal is to place five chips in a row—across, up or down, or diagonal—on the chart.

6 Players continue taking turns. The first player to get five chips in a row wins the game.

Players: 2

You'll Need

★ 100 Chart

★ half sheet of paper

★ number cube

★ 15 plastic chips of one color for each player

Place the Numbers

This beginning place value activity provides children practice in identifying tens and ones in a two-digit number. Introduce this activity in a whole-class setting. Afterwards, divide the class into small groups and assign a student who has mastered this skill to lead each group.

HERE'S HOW

Distribute copies of the "What Are the Numbers?" recording sheet and the 100 Chart to children. Give each child two plastic chips. Tell children that you will call out a two-digit number and they have to write the number and find it on their 100 Chart.

Spin the Tens and Ones spinners. Read the number aloud as tens and ones; for example, "1 ten, 5 ones." Have children write the number on their recording sheet. Then have them use a chip to cover the number on their 100 Chart.

Next, ask children to reverse the place value of the digits and record the new number on their sheet; for example, "5 tens, 1 one, 51." Then have them cover that number with a chip on their 100 Chart as well. Ask children to compare the two numbers: *Is the first number greater than or less than the second number? Or are the two numbers equal? How do you know?* Have them write the correct symbol (>, <, or =) between the numbers on their recording sheet. Repeat the activity a few more times to help children gain a better understanding of tens and ones.

MATERIALS

- **What Are the Numbers? recording sheet (page 32)**
- **100 Chart (page 62)**
- **Tens and Ones spinners (page 63)**
- **plastic chips**
- **Place the Numbers game directions (page 33), optional**

VARIATION

Have children do the activity in small groups, with each child taking turns spinning, verbalizing, and recording the tens/ones names, and comparing the numbers. Give each group a copy of the "Place the Numbers" game directions.

Name: _____ Date: _____

What Are the Numbers?

Spin to make a two-digit number. Write the number below. Then switch its place values and write the new number. Compare the two numbers. Write >, <, or =.

Tens	Ones	Number	greater than (>), less than (<), or equal (=)	Tens	Ones	Number
1	5	15	<	5	1	51

Place the Numbers

Work together to name numbers using their place value.

What to Do

1 One player spins the Tens and Ones spinners. The player reads aloud the tens number and the ones number; for example, "1 ten, 5 ones."

2 All players write the number on their recording sheet. Then they use a chip to cover that number on their own 100 Chart.

3 Next, the first player switches the place value of the digits. The player says the new number aloud; for example, "5 tens, 1 one."

4 All players record the new number on their sheet. Then they cover the number on their chart.

5 Compare the two numbers. Is the first number greater than or less than the second number? Or are the two numbers equal? Players record >, <. or = on their sheet.

6 The next player takes a turn. Repeat Steps 1 to 5.

7 Continue until all players have had at least one turn spinning the spinners.

Players: 2 to 4

You'll Need

★ Tens and Ones spinners

★ What Are the Numbers? recording sheet for each player

★ 100 Chart for each player

★ plastic chips

Egg-Carton Toss

This active small-group game is perfect for a math center! It might take a little time to make the Egg-Carton 100 Chart, but it is well worth it for the fun factor!

To make the Egg-Carton 100 Chart, collect ten empty egg cartons. Cut off the two end holes to turn each carton into a 2-by-5 array.* Arrange the egg cartons into columns to form a 10-by-10 array on a table. Grab some lightweight game pieces (such as plastic linking cubes or small beanbags), and children are ready to play!

* You can also use these cartons as hands-on ten frames, which are great for learning how to compose and decompose small numbers.

HERE'S HOW

Put the Egg-Carton 100 Chart on a table. Use masking tape to mark a spot a couple of feet back from the end of the table. This will be the "throw line."

To play the game, have players line up behind the throw line. At his or her turn, a player tosses a game piece into an egg hole. (Tell children that a light underhand toss works best.) The player tries to identify the number that hole corresponds to on the 100 Chart. If correct, the player gets two points. If the player can also give the number in expanded notation (for example, 3 tens and 4 ones, or 30 + 4), award two bonus points for a total of four points. Record the player's points on the scoring sheet. Game continues until each player has made ten tosses. Add up the points to determine the winner.

VARIATIONS

- Arranged in columns, the egg cartons make an obvious odd/even pattern. Play the game as above using this revised scoring system: If a player's game piece lands in an odd-numbered hole, the ones digit is the number of points scored. If the toss lands in an even-numbered hole, the tens digit is the number of points scored. The first player whose points add up to 100 wins.

- Arranged in rows, the cartons make it easy to find multiples of 5. Have players take turns trying to toss a game piece into a hole representing a multiple of 5. Players receive the number of points corresponding to the value on the 100 Chart, but only when it is a multiple of 5. The first player to reach a total score of 300 wins.

MATERIALS

- Egg-Carton 100 Chart (see instructions above)
- masking tape
- 10 game pieces in one color for each player
- Egg-Carton Toss scoring sheet (page 36)
- 100 Chart (page 62), optional

Egg-Carton Toss

Toss game pieces into the Egg-Carton 100 Chart to win points.

What to Do

1 Assign one player to keep score for everyone. Give that player the Egg-Carton Toss scoring sheet.

2 Players stand in line behind the throw line.

3 The first player tosses a game piece into an egg hole. Use a gentle underhand toss for best results.

4 The player has to say the number that hole matches to on the 100 Chart. If correct, the player gets two points.

BONUS **If the player can also say the number in expanded notation (for example, 3 tens and 4 ones or 30 + 4), he or she gets two more points.**

5 The scorekeeper records the points on the scoring sheet.

6 The next player takes a turn. Repeat Steps 3 to 5.

7 After every player has made ten tosses, the scorekeeper adds up the scores.

8 The player with the most points wins.

Players: 3 to 5

You'll Need

★ Egg-Carton 100 Chart

★ 10 game pieces in one color for each player

★ Egg-Carton Toss scoring sheet

★ 100 Chart

Egg-Carton Toss

Write players' names on the top row. Then record each player's score below his or her name.

Players					
1					
2					
3					
4					
5					
6					
7					
8					
9					
10					
Total					

Guess the Number

In this version of "20 Questions," children try to identify a number from 1 to 100. The goal is to help them move from simply guessing the number to using effective questioning strategies to find the answer. Introduce this game in a whole-class setting to model good questioning. Encourage children to ask a variety of question types, not just "more or less" questions. As they become more proficient in logical thinking and listening skills, you will notice it takes fewer questions for them to find the correct answer. Afterwards, you can divide the class into small groups to play the game.

HERE'S HOW

Distribute copies of the 100 Chart to children, as well as plastic chips. Explain to children that in this game they will try to guess a number from 1 to 100 by asking questions about it. Tell them to ask yes or no questions that will help narrow down the possible answers; for example: *Is 5 one of the digits? Does it have 3 tens? Is it even? Is it less than 50?*

To play, spin the Tens and Ones spinners to get a number from 1 to 100. (Use 00 for 100.) Invite children to ask questions to guess the number. Remind them to use good questioning strategies. Have children keep track of their guesses by covering numbers on their 100 Chart with plastic chips. For example, if the answer to "Does it have 3 tens?" is "No," they should cover all the numbers that have 3 tens on their chart to eliminate them. If no one has guessed the number after 20 questions, reveal the number.

MATERIALS

- 100 Chart (page 62)
- Tens and Ones spinners (page 63)
- plastic chips

VARIATION

Have children play the game in small groups, with each player taking a turn spinning to get the secret number and answering other players' questions.

Guess the Number

Ask questions to guess a number from 1 to 100.

What to Do

1 One player spins the Tens and Ones spinners to get a number. (OO means 100.) Keep the number a secret!

2 The other players take turns asking yes or no questions to guess the number. For example: "Is 5 one of the digits?" "Is it even?"

3 After each question, players use their chips to help them keep track of possible answers. For example, say the answer to "Is 5 one of the digits?" is "no." Players cover all the numbers with 5 on their 100 Chart to get rid of them.

4 Players work together to guess the number. Try to guess the number in 20 questions or less!

5 If no one guesses the number after 20 questions, the first player tells the secret number.

6 The next player takes a turn. Repeat Steps 1 to 5.

7 Game continues until every player has had a turn spinning to get the secret number.

Players: 3 to 5

You'll Need
- ★ Tens and Ones spinners
- ★ 100 Chart for each player
- ★ plastic chips

Battleship

Playing this version of the game "Battleship" on a 100 Chart is a fun way for children to practice adding and subtracting tens and ones, using expanded notation, recognizing patterns, and problem solving.

HERE'S HOW

Pair up children and give each player two laminated 100 Charts, 16 plastic chips, and a dry-erase marker. Place a divider between the players to hide their "battleships." Have each player lay out four battleships on one of the charts by placing four chips in a row, either vertically or horizontally, for each battleship. Tell players they'll use the second 100 Chart and dry-erase marker to record hits and misses.

To play the game, Player 1 names a number on the 100 Chart, using both expanded form and number name; for example, "30 and 5, 35." If there is a battleship on that number on Player 2's board, she says, "Hit." If there is no battleship on that number, Player 2 says, "Miss." Player 1 records the hit or miss on his second 100 Chart, using O's (circling the numbers) for hits and X's for misses. Player 2 takes a turn, repeating the same procedure.

Players continue taking turns naming numbers and recording hits and misses. You may want to share the strategy that if they "hit" a number, they might want to try the numbers right next to it (to its left or right, or above or below it) to determine the location of the entire battleship. Explain that a battleship is sunk when all four numbers in the battleship have been hit. The game ends when one player has sunk all of the other player's battleships.

MATERIALS

(for each player)

- 2 laminated 100 Charts (page 62)
- dry-erase marker
- 16 plastic chips
- cardboard, manila folder, or large book to use as a divider (for each pair of players)

Battleship

Play a game of Battleship on the 100 Chart! Use what you know about tens and ones to find and sink your opponent's battleships.

What to Do

1 Place a divider between players. Each player puts a 100 Chart behind the divider to hide his or her "battleships."

2 Each player makes four battleships on the hidden 100 Chart. To make a battleship, place four chips in a row—vertically (up and down) or horizontally (left to right).

3 Player 1 says a number to guess where Player 2 might have a battleship. Use expanded form and the number's name; for example, "30 and 5, 35."

- If Player 2 has a battleship on that number, she says, "Hit." Player 1 circles the number on his other 100 Chart to record a hit.

- If there is no battleship on that number, Player 2 says, "Miss." Player 1 marks that number with an X.

4 Player 2 takes a turn guessing a number.

5 Players continue taking turns guessing numbers and recording hits and misses.

6 A battleship is sunk when all four of its numbers have been "hit." The game ends when one player has sunk all of the other player's battleships.

Players: 2

You'll Need
(for each player)
- ★ 2 laminated 100 Charts
- ★ dry-erase marker
- ★ 16 plastic chips
- ★ cardboard, manila folder, or large book to use as a divider

Race to 100

This simple 2- or 3-player game is a favorite with young learners. The 100 Chart helps support children in learning to add larger numbers, as they can use the patterns they have learned there to become more fluent with addition. Perfect for your math center!

HERE'S HOW

Put children in pairs or in groups of three. Give each group a 100 Chart, a Ones spinner, and a different-colored plastic chip for each player.

To play the game, the first player spins the spinner to get a number. Starting at 1, the player moves forward that many spaces on the 100 Chart and places her chip on the number. The player should say the addition sentence that describes the move. For example, say she spins a 5. As she moves forward 5 spaces, she says aloud, "1 + 5 = 6." The next player takes a turn using a chip of another color, and so on. Players continue taking turns spinning the spinner and adding the number where they land to their previous number. The first player to pass 100 on the chart wins the game.

MATERIALS

- 100 Chart* (page 62)
- Ones spinner (page 63)
- different-colored plastic chip for each player
- Color to 100 activity page (page 43), optional

* You may want to laminate the 100 Chart for durability.

VARIATION

Have children play "Color to 100" on their own or with a partner. In this twist to "Race to 100," children tally the number of spins it takes them to get to 100. After they spin to get a number, children color that many spaces on their own 100 Chart using a different color each time. This helps them check that their tally is correct.

Race to 100

Spin the spinner and add to reach 100 first.

What to Do

1 Players take turns spinning the spinner. The player who spins the highest number goes first.

2 Player 1 spins the spinner to get a number. Starting at 1, the player moves forward that number of spaces on the 100 Chart. Player 1 places a chip on that number.

3 Player 1 should say the addition sentence that describes his move. For example, say he spins a 5. As he moves forward 5 spaces, he says, "1 + 5 = 6."

4 The next player takes a turn, using a chip of a different color. Repeat Steps 2 and 3.

5 Players continue taking turns.

6 The first player to pass 100 on the 100 Chart wins the game.

Players: 2 or 3

You'll Need

★ Ones spinner

★ 100 Chart

★ different-colored plastic chip for each player

Name: _____   Date: _____

Color to 100

Spin the spinner and color the spaces to get to 100!

What to Do

1 Spin the spinner. Write the number you spun below.

2 Color in that number of spaces on your 100 Chart.

3 Make a tally mark each time you spin.

4 Keep spinning and coloring until you have colored to 100! Use a different color for each spin.

> **You'll Need**
> ★ Ones spinner
> ★ Blank 100 Chart
> ★ pencil
> ★ crayons

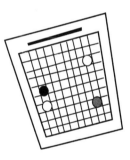

Number Spun Record the number you get at each spin.	Tally Make a tally mark each time you spin. How many spins did it take to get to 100?

Race From 100

Played like "Race to 100," only backwards, this 2- or 3-player game provides children with an opportunity to use the 100 Chart to practice subtraction with larger numbers. Children can use the pattern relationships they already know to help them as they subtract.

Put children in pairs or in groups of three. Give each group a 100 Chart, a Ones spinner, and a different-colored plastic chip for each player. Tell children that in this game, they will be moving backward on the 100 Chart.

To play the game, the first player spins the spinner to get a number. Starting at 100, the player moves back that many spaces on the 100 Chart. The player then places her chip on the number where she lands. The player also says the subtraction sentence that describes her move. For example, if the player spins a 5, she says, "100 – 5 = 95." The next player takes a turn using a chip of another color. Players continue taking turns, subtracting the number they spun from their previous difference. The first player to pass number 1 on the 100 Chart wins the game.

- 100 Chart* (page 62)
- Ones spinner (page 63)
- different-colored plastic chip for each player

* You may want to laminate the 100 Chart for durability.

Race From 100

Spin the spinner and subtract to reach 1 first.

What to Do

1 Players take turns spinning the spinner. The player who spins the highest number goes first.

2 Player 1 spins the spinner to get a number. Starting at 100, the player moves back that number of spaces on the 100 Chart. Player 1 places a chip on the number where she lands.

3 Player 1 should say the subtraction sentence that describes her move. For example, if Player 1 spins a 5, she says, "100 – 5 = 95."

4 The next player takes a turn, using a chip of a different color. Repeat Steps 2 and 3.

5 Players continue taking turns.

6 The first player to pass number 1 on the 100 Chart wins the game.

Players: 2 or 3

You'll Need

★ 100 Chart

★ Ones spinner

★ different-colored plastic chip for each player

What's the Sum?

Adding consecutive numbers on a hundred chart reveals many patterns. In this activity, children look for patterns as they add two, three, or four consecutive numbers. This is a great way to provide children with authentic practice in multiple-digit addition.

HERE'S HOW

Distribute copies of the 100 Chart to children. Demonstrate a few examples of adding consecutive numbers in a consecutive set (see below). Explain to children that they can start anywhere on the 100 Chart. Then have them try the following variations. (Allow them to use calculators, if necessary.)

- Have children add two consecutive numbers, then continue adding the next two consecutive numbers in a row to make at least five or six sets of consecutive numbers in order to identify any patterns that result.

MATERIALS

- 100 Chart (page 62)
- paper or math journal
- pencil
- calculators (optional)

Adding 2 consecutive numbers	Sum	Pattern
1 + 2	3	
3 + 4	7	+ 4
5 + 6	11	+ 4
7 + 8	15	+ 4
9 + 10	19	+ 4
11 + 12	23	+ 4

- Have children add three consecutive numbers, then continue adding the next three consecutive numbers to make at least five or six sets of consecutive numbers in order to identify any patterns that result.

Adding 3 consecutive numbers	Sum	Pattern
1 + 2 + 3	6	
4 + 5 + 6	15	+ 9
7 + 8 + 9	24	+ 9
10 + 11 + 12	33	+ 9
13 + 14 + 15	42	+ 9
16 + 17 + 18	51	+ 9

What's the Sum?
(continued)

- Have children add four consecutive numbers, then continue adding the next four consecutive numbers to make at least five or six sets of consecutive numbers in order to identify any patterns that result.

Adding 4 consecutive numbers	Sum	Pattern
1 + 2 + 3 + 4	10	
5 + 6 + 7 + 8	26	+ 16
9 + 10 + 11 + 12	42	+ 16
13 + 14 + 15 + 16	58	+ 16
17 + 18 + 19 + 20	74	+ 16
21 + 22 + 23 + 24	90	+ 16

Guide children to notice that adding two consecutive numbers repeatedly results in a difference of 4 (or 2 squared) between each set of numbers. Adding three consecutive numbers repeatedly results in a difference of 9 (or 3 squared) between each set. Adding four consecutive numbers repeatedly results in a difference of 16 (or 4 squared) between each set. Ask children: *What do you think will happen when you add five consecutive numbers?* (The difference between each set will be 25, or 5 squared.)

Name: _____ Date: _____

What's the Sum?

Add several numbers in a row. See if you can find a pattern.

What to Do

Choose one of these versions. Record the numbers on a sheet of paper or in your math journal.

Version 1: Add two consecutive numbers (two numbers in a row). Then add the next two numbers in a row. Continue adding two consecutive numbers until you have about six sets.

Version 2: Add three consecutive numbers (three numbers in a row). Then add the next three numbers in a row. Continue adding three consecutive numbers until you have about six sets.

Version 3: Add four consecutive numbers (four numbers in a row). Then add the next four numbers in a row. Continue adding four consecutive numbers until you have about six sets.

You'll Need
★ 100 Chart
★ pencil
★ paper or math journal
★ calculator (optional)

Finished? Great! Now do this:

- Find another place to start on the 100 Chart. Make about six sets of consecutive-number sums.
- Do this at least one more time!
- Can you see any patterns in your work?
- Try a different version. Do you see any similarities or differences in the patterns?

Innies and Outies

This is one of my favorite ways to give more advanced students extra practice with multi-digit addition! Children pick any four consecutive numbers—in rows, columns, or diagonals—on the 100 Chart, then add the inner numbers and outer numbers. It's a simple procedure, but the results motivate children to repeat the activity several times, giving them lots of fun, purposeful practice. Have children do this activity individually or in pairs.

Distribute copies of the 100 Chart to children, as well as paper and pencil.

Tell children to choose any four consecutive numbers in a row on the chart. Then ask them to find the sum of the two outer numbers (outies) and the sum of the two inner numbers (innies). Have them record the numbers and sums on their paper. Have children do this several times using consecutive numbers in rows, then in columns and diagonals. Ask: *What pattern do you see in the sums?* (The sum of the innies equals the sum of the outies.)

- 100 Chart (page 62)
- paper or math journal
- pencil
- calculators (optional)

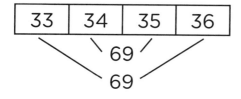

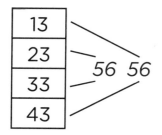

Name: _____ Date: _____

Innies and Outies

**Pick four numbers in a row. Add the innies and the outies.
What do you notice?**

What to Do

1 On your 100 Chart, choose any four
consecutive numbers in a row (across).

2 Write the four numbers on a piece of paper.

3 Find the sum of the two outer numbers
(outies).

4 Find the sum of the two inner numbers
(innies).

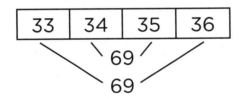

5 Choose another four consecutive numbers. Repeat Steps 2 to 4.
Do this again several times.

6 Next, choose any four consecutive numbers in a column
(up and down). Repeat Steps 2 to 5.

7 Finally, choose any four numbers in diagonals (/ or \).
Repeat Steps 2 to 5.

8 Do you see any patterns? What patterns do you see?

9 Can you find any innies and outies that don't follow the pattern?

> ### You'll Need
> ★ 100 Chart
> ★ paper or math
>   journal
> ★ pencil
> ★ calculators

Boxes

"Boxes" is another activity that provides children with authentic multi-digit addition practice. Children draw a square box around any set of numbers on the 100 Chart. They add opposite corners of the box and look for patterns in the sums. Doing this activity with a 10-by-10 array provides an opportunity to broaden the lesson to explore sums in an arithmetic series, one of Carl Friedrich Gauss's early mathematical discoveries. Anecdotal evidence points to this discovery being made while he was in elementary school!

HERE'S HOW

Distribute laminated copies of the 100 Chart to children.

Using dry-erase markers, have children draw a square box around any numbers on the chart, starting with a 2-by-2 array. Ask children to add the two numbers in opposite corners of the box and record their sum. Then have them do the same with the numbers in the remaining two opposite corners. Encourage children to try this several times to identify any patterns.

Next, have children draw larger boxes, working with 3-by-3, 4-by-4, 5-by-5, and even larger arrays. Encourage them to try each array size several times to determine if any patterns exist.

14	15
24	25

14 + 25 = 39

15 + 24 = 39

66	67	68
76	77	78
86	87	88

66 + 88 = 154

68 + 86 = 154

MATERIALS

- laminated 100 Chart (page 62)
- dry-erase markers
- paper or math journals
- pencils
- calculators (optional)

VARIATION

This variation will provide practice with adding more than two multi-digit numbers. Ask children to draw a square array of any size 3-by-3 or greater on the 100 Chart. Have them add the numbers in one diagonal of the array. Then have them add the numbers in the opposite diagonal and compare both sums.

Name: _____   Date: _____

Boxes

Draw square boxes on the 100 Chart. Then add the numbers on each box's opposite corners. What do you notice?

What to Do

1 On the 100 Chart, draw a square box around any group of four numbers (a 2-by-2 array).

2 Add the two numbers in opposite corners. Then add the two numbers in the other two opposite corners. Record the sums on a sheet of paper or in your math journal.

3 Draw several other 2-by-2 arrays on the 100 Chart. Repeat Step 2 each time. Do you notice any patterns?

4 Next, draw 3-by-3 arrays (square boxes around any group of nine numbers). Repeat Step 2 each time. Do you notice any patterns?

5 You can do this with 4-by-4, 5-by-5, or larger arrays. Remember: Try each size array many times to see if there is a pattern.

> **You'll Need**
> ★ laminated 100 Chart
> ★ dry-erase marker
> ★ paper or math journal
> ★ pencil
> ★ calculator (optional)

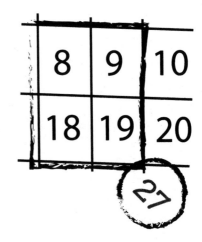

Variation

Draw a square array of any size on the 100 Chart. Add all the numbers in one diagonal (/) of the array. Then add all the numbers in the other diagonal of the array (\). Record the sums. Do this several times. What do you notice?

Crosses

In this activity, children look for patterns in the sums of numbers surrounding a chosen number. More advanced students can also take this opportunity to practice multi-digit multiplication and check it using addition.

HERE'S HOW

Distribute copies of the 100 Chart to children. Have children choose any number on the chart and add it four times (or for more advanced students, multiply it by 4). Then have them add the four numbers in the row and in the column that surround that number (see below). In other words, have them add the two numbers above and the two numbers below the chosen number. Then have them add the two numbers to the left and the two numbers to the right of the chosen number. Ask children: *What do you notice about the sums?*

		13		
		23		
31	32	33	34	35
		43		
		53		

$33 + 33 + 33 + 33 = 33 \times 4 = 132$

$13 + 23 + 43 + 53 = 132$

$31 + 32 + 34 + 35 = 132$

Encourage students to do the same with several different numbers on the 100 Chart. At the end of the activity, take time for discussion, asking questions such as: *What are the sums? Do you see a pattern? What is it?*

MATERIALS

- **100 Chart (page 62)**
- paper
- pencils
- calculators (optional)

VARIATION

Have children try this activity using the numbers in diagonals. Ask: *Is the pattern similar to that of the crosses?*

23				27
	34		36	
		45		
	54		56	
63				67

$45 + 45 + 45 + 45 = 45 \times 4 = 180$

$23 + 34 + 56 + 67 = 180$

$27 + 36 + 54 + 63 = 180$

Name: _____ Date: _____

Crosses

Pick a number. Then add the numbers around it. Is there a pattern?

What to Do

1 Choose any number on the 100 Chart. Add it four times (or multiply it by 4).

2 Now add the two numbers above and the two numbers below your chosen number. (For example, say you chose the number 33. Add 13 + 23 + 43 + 53.) What is the sum of those four numbers?

You'll Need

★ 100 Chart

★ paper

★ pencil

★ calculator (optional)

3 Next, add the two numbers to the left and the two numbers to the right of your chosen number. (For example, add 31 + 32 + 34 + 35.) What is the sum?

		13		
		23		
31	32	33	34	35
		43		
		53		

4 Repeat Steps 1 to 3 at least three more times. Choose a different number each time. Do you see a pattern? What is it?

Variation

Choose a number from the 100 Chart. This time, add the two numbers above and the two numbers below in the diagonals (\ /). Do you see a pattern here?

Patterns in Multiples

This activity is not meant to be completed in one class period, but is rather ongoing, allowing children time to explore patterns. Looking at patterns made by counting multiples can help children develop meaning in multiplication and division. They can discover applications for the commutative, associative, and distributive properties, helping them develop fluency with basic facts. They can determine the factors of numbers. There is no single general strategy for multiplying or dividing single-digit numbers. However, depending on the number, children may discover a few strategies for themselves by skip-counting multiples and highlighting them on the 100 Chart. Follow up with a whole-class discussion about patterns they found.

HERE'S HOW

Distribute copies of the 100 Chart and highlighters, crayons, or plastic chips to children. Display a copy of the chart on the board. Decide what number you want to focus on and invite children to find multiples of that number on their 100 Chart. Have them color or cover the multiples with transparent chips. Afterwards, guide children in a discussion about patterns they might discover as they color or cover numbers on the chart.

Multiples of 2: Work with children to identify the first 20 multiples of 2 and discuss their observations. Then have them complete the pattern on their own 100 Chart. Some pattern rules children might observe include:

• All the numbers are even. Ask: *What does "even" mean?*

• Multiples of 2 have a 0, 2, 4, 6, or 8 in the ones place.

• There are 50 multiples of 2 in 100, so 50 × 2 = 100.

Multiples of 10: Observations might include:

• Multiples of 10 are arranged in a single column.

• Multiples of 10 have a 0 in the ones place.

• There are 10 multiples of 10 in 100, so 10 × 10 = 100.

Multiples of 5: Have children work on the same 100 Chart they used for multiples of 10. Observations might include:

• There are twice as many multiples of 5 as there are of 10, so 20 × 5 = 100.

• Multiples of 5 are arranged in two columns.

• Multiples of 5 have 0 or 5 in the ones place.

MATERIALS

• 100 Chart (page 62)

• colored highlighters, crayons, or transparent plastic chips

• classroom projection system or hundred wall chart and markers

(continued)

Patterns in Multiples
(continued)

Multiples of 3: Observations might include:

• There are three colored squares in the first two rows, followed by four colored squares in the third row. This pattern repeats as they go down the 100 Chart.

• This is a "skip-two" pattern.

• Not every number that ends in 3 is a multiple of 3.

• There are diagonal patterns in multiples of 3.

• Going down the diagonals of 3, 6, and 9, the tens increase by one ten and the ones decrease by one.

• The sum of the digits in each number in the "3" diagonal is 3.

• The sum of the digits in each number in the "6" diagonal is 6.

• The sum of the digits in each number in the "9" diagonal is 9.

100 Chart

1	2	3	4	5	6	7	8	9	10
11	12	13	14	15	16	17	18	19	20
21	22	23	24	25	26	27	28	29	30
31	32	33	34	35	36	37	38	39	40
41	42	43	44	45	46	47	48	49	50
51	52	53	54	55	56	57	58	59	60
61	62	63	64	65	66	67	68	69	70
71	72	73	74	75	76	77	78	79	80
81	82	83	84	85	86	87	88	89	90
91	92	93	94	95	96	97	98	99	100

To introduce identifying factors, explain how to determine the **digital root** of a number. Simply add all the digits in a number repeatedly until you reach a single digit. (For example, take the number 66. Adding its digits results in 12; adding these digits, in turn, results in 3. So the digital root of 66 is 3.) Children may then discover that each number in the 3, 6, and 9 diagonals sums to 3, 6, and 9 respectively. Using digital roots is a quick way to determine if 3, 6, or 9 is a factor. If the digital root is 3, the number is divisible by 3. If the digital root is 9, then the number is divisible by 3 and 9. If the digital root is 6 and the number is even, then 3 and 6 are factors.

Multiples of 4: Observations might include:

• There are half as many multiples of 4 as there are of 2. This relates to the fact that 4 is equal to 2 groups of 2 ($4 = 2 \times 2$).

• If you divide a number by 2 once and it results in an even number, then the number must be divisible by 4.

Multiples of 8: After finding multiples of 4, have children use the same 100 Chart to find multiples of 8. Their discoveries will be similar:

• There are half as many multiples of 8 as there are of 4, which is half as many as 2. Related fact: $8 = 2 \times 2 \times 2$.

• So, if you divide a number by 2 twice and it results in an even number, then the number must be divisible by 8.

Play & Learn Math: Hundred Chart © Susan Andrews Kunze, Scholastic Inc.

Choose & Multiply

This 2- or 3-player game provides children with practice in basic multiplication facts. Players spin a spinner three times to get three numbers. They then decide which of the numbers to multiply together to get a product. The goal is to get a number that is not already covered on the 100 Chart. Strategy is important in this game, which just adds to the fun!

HERE'S HOW

Put children in pairs or in groups of three. Give each group a 100 Chart, a Ones spinner, and 10 plastic chips of one color for each player.

To play the game, the first player spins the spinner three times and records the numbers on his paper or math journal. (Use 0 for 10.) He then chooses two or three of the numbers to make a multiplication sentence. For example, if the player spins 3, 4, and 6, he could choose to make any one of these sentences: 3 × 4 = 12, 3 × 6 = 18, 4 × 6 = 24, or 3 × 4 × 6 = 72. The player records his sentence of choice, then covers the product with a chip on the 100 Chart. The next player takes a turn.

Only one chip can be in each number space. If a player cannot place her chip on the chart, the player must pass. Play continues until one player has placed all ten chips or all players have passed in one round.

MATERIALS

- laminated 100 Chart (page 62)
- Ones spinner (page 63)
* 10 plastic chips of one color for each player
- paper or math journal
- pencil

Choose & Multiply

Spin to get three numbers. Choose which numbers to multiply. Then cover the product on the 100 Chart.

What to Do

1. Players take turns spinning the spinner. The player who gets the highest number goes first.

2. Player 1 spins the spinner three times to get three numbers. (Use 0 for 10.) The player writes the numbers on his paper or math journal.

3. Player 1 chooses two or three of the numbers to make a multiplication sentence. For example, If the player rolls 3, 4, and 6, he can choose any of these sentences:

   $3 \times 4 = 12$ $3 \times 6 = 18$
   $4 \times 6 = 24$ $3 \times 4 \times 6 = 72$

4. Player 1 records his number sentence. Then he covers the product on the 100 Chart with a chip.

5. The next player takes a turn, repeating Steps 2 to 4. If a chip is already on a number, the player must pass.

6. Play continues until one player has placed all ten chips on the chart or all players pass in one round. The first player to place all his or her chips on the chart wins.

Players: 2 or 3

You'll Need

★ Ones spinner

★ 100 Chart

★ 10 plastic chips of one color for each player

★ paper or math journal

★ pencil

Dividing Evenly

In this activity, children use the 100 Chart to explore division. They count equal groups and subtract these equal groups multiple times to reach the answer to a division problem.

HERE'S HOW

Distribute copies of the "Keep Subtracting" activity page, the 100 Chart, and plastic chips to children. Display a copy of "Keep Subtracting" on the board.

Tell children that they will be solving division problems using subtraction and the 100 Chart to help them. Using the example on the activity page, model how to do just that. For example, you might say, *"Our problem is 24 ÷ 8. Starting at 24, let's subtract 8 from that number. What do we get? (16) Next, we'll subtract 8 from 16. What's the difference? (8) Finally we subtract 8 again to get to 0. How many times did we subtract 8 from 24? (3 times) That means there are 3 equal groups of 8 in 24, so 24 ÷ 8 = 3."*

Have children complete the activity sheet on their own or with a partner. Allow children to use chips on their 100 Chart to keep track of each subtraction step. By counting the chips at the end of each problem, children can check their answers. Make sure they record each subtraction step, counting the number of groups.

TIP

Working in pairs can help struggling children succeed with this activity.

MATERIALS

- **Keep Subtracting activity page (page 60)**
- **100 Chart (page 62)**
- **plastic chips**
- **classroom projection system**

VARIATION

For more advanced students, you can assign numbers that don't divide evenly. For example:

34 ÷ 8

34 – 8 = 26 (*1*)

26 – 8 = 18 (*2*)

18 – 8 = 10 (*3*)

10 – 8 = 2 (*r 2*)

34 ÷ 8 = 3 r 2

Name: _____ Date: _____

Keep Subtracting

Solve the division problems by subtracting equal groups. Count how many equal groups. Use plastic chips on the 100 Chart to mark each subtraction step. Then count the chips on the chart to check your answer.

For example: **24 ÷ 8**
24 – 8 = 16   *(1st equal group)*
16 – 8 = 8   *(2nd equal group)*
8 – 8 = 0   *(3rd equal group)*
24 ÷ 8 = 3 equal groups

1. 18 ÷ 3	**5.** 99 ÷ 11
2. 65 ÷ 5	**6.** 65 ÷ 13
3. 72 ÷ 9	**7.** 72 ÷ 18
4. 30 ÷ 10	**8.** 57 ÷ 19

Blank 100 Chart

100 Chart

1	2	3	4	5	6	7	8	9	10
11	12	13	14	15	16	17	18	19	20
21	22	23	24	25	26	27	28	29	30
31	32	33	34	35	36	37	38	39	40
41	42	43	44	45	46	47	48	49	50
51	52	53	54	55	56	57	58	59	60
61	62	63	64	65	66	67	68	69	70
71	72	73	74	75	76	77	78	79	80
81	82	83	84	85	86	87	88	89	90
91	92	93	94	95	96	97	98	99	100

Tens and Ones Spinners

To make a two-digit number, spin the Tens Spinner and the Ones Spinner. For example, if you spin a 7 in the Tens Spinner and a 3 in the Ones Spinner, you made 73. If you spin 0 in both spinners, you made 100.

Place a pencil and a paper clip at the center of a spinner, as shown. Flick the paper clip to spin the spinner.

Answer Key

Fill the Blocks (page 15)

1.

		5
	14	15
23	24	25
	34	35
		45

2.

54	55		
64	65		
74	75	76	77
		86	87

3.

36	37	38	39	40
46	47	48		
56	57			
66	67			

4.

		65				
	74	75	76			
83	84	85	86	87		
92	93	94	95	96	97	98

5.

31		33		35		37		39
	42		44		46		48	

Follow the Arrows (page 17)

1. 42   **2.** 24   **3.** 56   **4.** 68
5. 86   **6.** 74   **7.** 39   **8.** 55

Draw the Arrows (page 19)
Answers will vary. Possible answers:

1. ↘ ↘ ↘
2. ← ↘ ← ↘
3. → → ↗ → → ↘ →
4. ↑ ↑ ↑ ↑
5. ← ← ← ↘ ← ← ←
6. ↙ ↓ ↓
7. ↗ ↗ ↗ ↗ ↗ ↗
8. ← ← ↗ ← ← ← ↘

Next Numbers (page 24)

Starting Number	Rule	What Numbers Come Next?		
21	+5	26	31	36
83	-6	77	71	65
17	+10	27	37	47
48	-7	41	34	27
28	+9	37	46	55
97	-10	87	77	67
17	+8	25	33	41
88	-11	77	66	55
18	+20	38	58	78
75	-8	67	59	51
22	+11	33	44	55

Keep Subtracting (page 60)

1. 6   **2.** 13   **3.** 8   **4.** 3
5. 9   **6.** 5   **7.** 4   **8.** 3